RESPONSES

LIFE, THE UNIVERSE AND YOU

Barbara Wintersgill with Janet Dyson

Longman

HOW TO ASSESS YOUR OWN WORK

You can do the following exercise as a group, or as individuals, or both. The purpose of the exercise is to help you think about what you are learning as you go along. You can do the following exercise after working through a section of the book, or just after one activity.

1 Choose FOUR items from list **A** and FOUR items from list **B** which best describe what you have been doing.

2 Write down the items you have chosen and briefly explain why you chose each one, giving an example from your work as an illustration of that item, if possible. (For example: 'I chose **A 1** because we spent a lot of time talking about what we would do if we were told to fight in a war. Trevor told us about his grandad who had been in prison because he was a pacifist in the last war, and what he told me made me think a lot.')

3 If you did **1** and **2** as a group activity . . . was there any item which the group agreed on which you would not have chosen for yourself? If so explain why, and say what item you would have chosen instead. Why do you think you disagreed with the group decision?

4 Write about, or talk about, any one part of the work you particularly enjoyed and say why.

5 Write about, or talk about, any part of the work you did not enjoy.

6 Of all the work you have done in this section, which piece do you think is the best? Say why.

A – general

1 We listened to and learnt from each other.
2 We expressed our opinions and supported these opinions with reasonable arguments.
3 We worked well together as a group.
4 We presented our ideas and information clearly in writing.
5 We presented ideas and information to others but NOT in writing.
6 We had to use our imagination.
7 We did some creative work which we were satisfied with.
8 We solved problems.
9 We had to make decisions.
10 We had to explain the meaning of texts (writings).
11 We had to explain the meaning of pictures.
12 We researched new information.
13 We had to apply facts we already knew to a new situation.

B – specialist

1 We had to be clear about our own opinions and beliefs.
2 We had to consider what things give life a sense of purpose and meaning.

3 We asked questions about other people's beliefs and feelings.
4 We discussed how important religion is to us.
5 We had to put ourselves into the place of another person in order to understand their point of view.
6 We felt we could respect each other's views, and the views of other people.
7 We found out that everything is not as it first appears.
8 We discussed who we would like to take as a model for our own behaviour.
9 Some/one of us changed their minds about something.
10 We understood why there can be different solutions to a problem.
11 We understood why religion is sometimes, or always, important in some people's lives.
12 We made some decisions about what things in life are really important to us.
13 We felt that in some situations it was not possible to make a judgement or reach a decision.
14 We felt that although we each reached a decision on a matter, as we got older and found out more, that opinion might change.

CONTENTS

How to assess your own work   2

1 That's life   4
2 Who am I?   10
3 Airport!   14
4 Times of trouble   18
5 What's the point?   26
6 Because it's there   28
7 Achievement   31
8 Potential   32
9 What's the answer?   38

GCSE notes for the teacher   45

1 THAT'S LIFE

DEEP THOUGHT

Fook composed himself.

'O Deep Thought Computer,' he said, 'the task we have designed you to perform is this. We want you tell us . . .' he paused, '. . . the Answer!'

'The Answer?' said Deep Thought. 'The Answer to what?'

'Life!' urged Fook.

'The Universe!' said Lunkwill.

'Everything!' they said in chorus.

Deep Thought paused for a moment's reflection.

'Tricky,' he said finally.

'But can you do it?'

Again, a significant pause.

'Yes,' said Deep Thought, 'I can do it.'

'There is an answer?' said Fook with breathless excitement.

'A simple answer?' added Lunkwill.

'Yes,' said Deep Thought. 'Life, the Universe, and Everything. There is an answer. But,' he added, 'I'll have to think about it . . . the programme will take me a little while to run.'

Fook glanced impatiently at his watch.

'How long?' he said.

'Seven and a half million years,' said Deep Thought.

(from *Hitch-hiker's Guide to the Galaxy* by Douglas Adams)

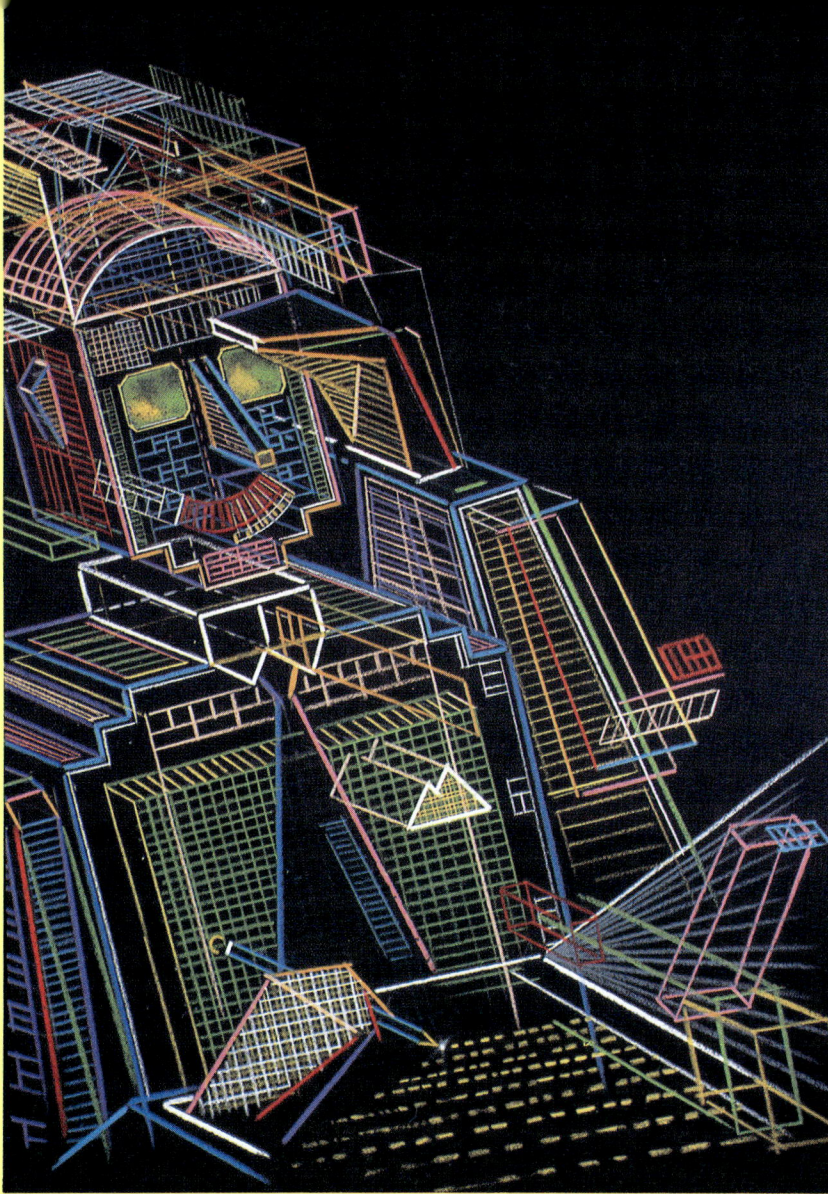

How do YOU see life? Do you just accept that things are as they are, or do you ask questions like the one Fook and Lunkwill were trying (very unsuccessfully!) to ask the computer? Many people do ask questions about 'Life, the Universe and You'; questions such as 'Why am I here?' 'Why am I like I am?' and 'What is the point of life?'

▷▷▶ GROUP WORK – QUESTION SWAP SHOP

In groups of three or four, write down four questions about 'Life, the Universe and You' which you think are the most puzzling. Swap your questions with those of another group. Now suggest answers to the other group's questions. Write their questions and your answers out neatly and display them for everyone to read.

Are there any questions which were asked by more than one group? If so, why do you think these questions were more popular than others?

THE WALL OF LIFE

People often make statements about life which tell us how they view life as a whole – or perhaps just how they feel about life at that moment.

Make a 'wall of life' as a class activity.

You will need . . .
a large area of wall covered with sugar paper
a number of card or sugar paper 'bricks' – 10 cm x 20 cm.

Write statements about life (either your own or those you have found in books) on the 'bricks' and make a wall out of them. It may take you some weeks to finish the wall – you can keep adding bricks for as long as you think of new ideas. Here are some examples to start you off.

LIFE IS AN INCURABLE DISEASE

LIFE IS VERY SWEET

Life is full of ups and downs

Human life is a state in which much has to be endured and little to be enjoyed

LIFE IS MOSTLY FROTH AND BUBBLE

LIFE IS REAL!

Life is just one damned thing after another

LIFE IS GOOD

Life is a bowl of cherries

DISCUSSING THE WALL

When you have finished the wall, read all the bricks carefully. Which of the statements about life are POSITIVE and which are NEGATIVE? Do some statements contain both positive and negative ideas?

Look at the POSITIVE statements. What do you think makes people make statements like these about life? Do you agree with any of them?

Now ask yourself the same questions about the negative statements.

THE·PICTURE GAME

This is a group and class activity. It can be played many times using different themes.

1 Play as a group. Each person has to find two pictures which illustrate what they think life is all about.

2 Lay all the pictures out on a table.

3 Each person in the group selects ONE of their own pictures, and ONE picture which someone else has brought in, and explains to the rest of the group in what ways those pictures say something to them about what life is all about.

4 Finally, all the groups come together. Each person explains to the rest of the class why ANOTHER PERSON in their group chose one of their pictures.

You can vary this game by using a different theme:
e.g. 'pictures which say most about the state of the world as it is' or 'pictures which say most about your hopes for the future'.

· THAT'S · LIFE ·

See how many themes you can think of.

Here are four pictures. By the side of each one someone has written about why they chose that picture to illustrate 'what life is all about'.

1

'This mask of the Buddha gives me a feeling of inner peace and calm. I like the discipline of Buddhism; the ability to focus your mind on the things that really matter, and to put all distractions and worries on one side for a time is something I would like to be able to do.'

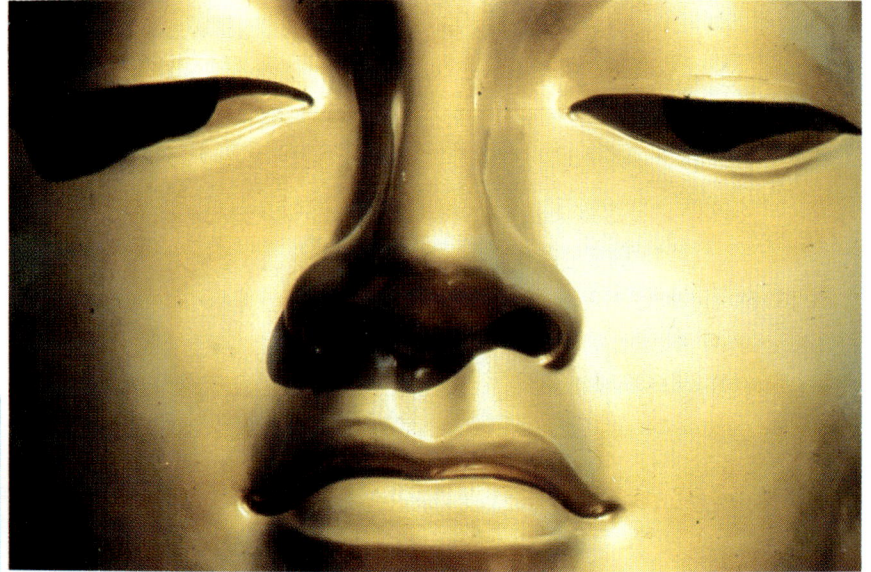

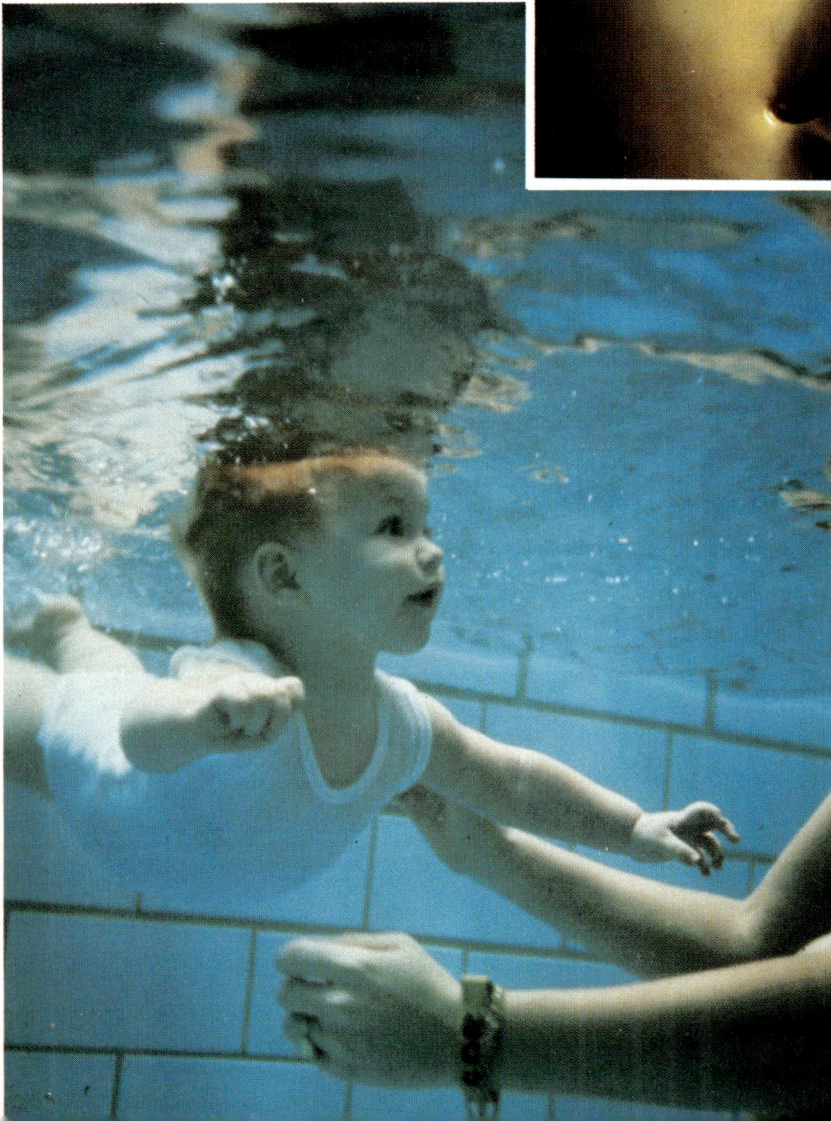

2

'I chose the baby swimming because it seemed to suggest all the possibilities that lie ahead of us at the beginning of our lives. The baby has her eyes open and looks quite unafraid – she obviously trusts the person who is holding her. The picture makes you realise how much humans depend on one another for support, help and love.'

3

'I have always been fascinated by the ideas of eternity and infinity – the idea that time goes on for ever, and that space goes on for ever. When I was very young, I used to look out of my bedroom window at night and gaze at the stars. I still do – and for some reason it gives me a comforting feeling. When I was small I used to imagine that far away, space and the stars and planets were contained in some sort of invisible box. But then the question always came into my mind "what is beyond the box?" The only answer can be "more space". It can never end. I'm not sure that it's possible to believe in the existence of nothing. It doesn't make sense. I couldn't bear to think that there is. I am sure that there must be other forms of life and other civilisations out there – and that gives me hope for the future. But above all, gazing into the sky for me puts us in our true perspective – it reminds me of how small and insignificant we all are, and how little we have achieved in comparison to the Universe.'

4

'This is a symbol of hope, adventure, achievement and tragedy. It stands for human beings' desire to keep asking questions and to keep finding out and inventing new things. But the terrible tragedy when seven astronauts were killed reminds me that however clever we think we are, we are not perfect.'

2 WHO AM I ?

- *THINK ABOUT WHAT MAKES A PERSON HUMAN, AND HOW HUMAN BEINGS ARE DIFFERENT FROM ANIMALS.*
- *FIND OUT ABOUT HOW ONE PERSON CAN APPEAR VERY DIFFERENT TO OTHER PEOPLE, AND THINK ABOUT HOW YOU SEE YOURSELF AND OTHERS – AND HOW THEY SEE YOU.*
- *THINK ABOUT WHAT SORT OF PEOPLE YOU ADMIRE.*

BEING HUMAN

Many people believe that human beings are very special in ways that other animals are not. Some people believe that human beings are in some way intended to be the 'image of God', and were specially made or chosen by God to fulfil some special purpose.

Here is a passage by Michael Grimmitt about turtles. Read it carefully.

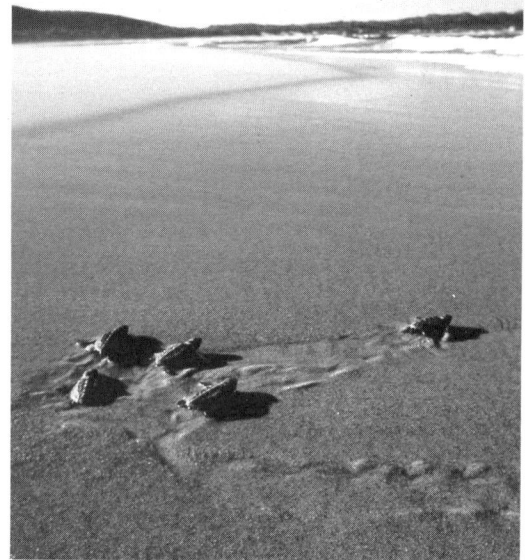

Humans versus turtles

Let us for a moment think about the life cycle of the turtle. When the female turtles have been fertilised, they come out of the sea, crawl up the beach and scoop deep holes in the sand. They each lay approximately two hundred eggs into their holes, cover them with sand and return to the sea. Days later, the eggs begin to hatch. From them emerge hundred of little turtles. Immediately they begin a dangerous journey to the sea. Many are picked off in the first few hours of life by seagulls, and many others fall victim to predators before they reach maturity. I understand that only four or five per cent of turtles actually reach maturity.

Infant turtles do not have to *learn* to be turtles; they *are* turtles. The turtle's nature is fixed; it is programmed to perform actions which are absolutely predictable right from the moment of birth until the moment of death. Like McDougall's self-raising flour, the quality of the turtle's life never varies. 'Turtlehood' provides no possibility for surprises. Like father, like son.

Grimmitt follows this with a passage describing humans, and showing ways in which they are not like turtles. Write your own passage on this theme.

WHO AM I?

'WHO AM I? . . . there are many people who would claim to be qualified to answer this question for me: a genealogist, a biologist, even an immigration control officer looking at my passport, could answer my question, "who am I?". But their answers would all be partial, fragmentary, incomplete. No one but myself can begin to deal with my wholeness, and the question "who am I?" is about my wholeness.'

(Michael Grimmitt)

SELF-PORTRAIT

1 Find out what *sort* of information the following people should be able to give about you. Also find out HOW they would get this information. Present your answers in a chart like the one on the right. (NB You do not have to say what the information *is*.)
   - a genealogist
   - a biologist
   - a psychologist
   - an immigration control officer.

2 The writer says that their information about you would be 'fragmentary' and 'incomplete'. What does this mean?

3 What sort of information about you might the following people be able to add:
   your best friend?   your parent?   your teacher?

4 What *sort* of information about yourself is known only to you?

THE WHOLE ME

Using a large sheet of paper or card, draw a diagram like the one on this page. You will see that around the figure of 'me' have been drawn some areas labelled with the name/title of a person or group who might say something about you. You can choose the people you want to include, but make sure that one of the spaces is headed 'ME'.

If you want to, you can write down in each space what that person or group of people say about you. (For example: under TEACHERS you might write down some comments from your last school report.)

When you have finished, display your work. Look at everyone else's pictures.

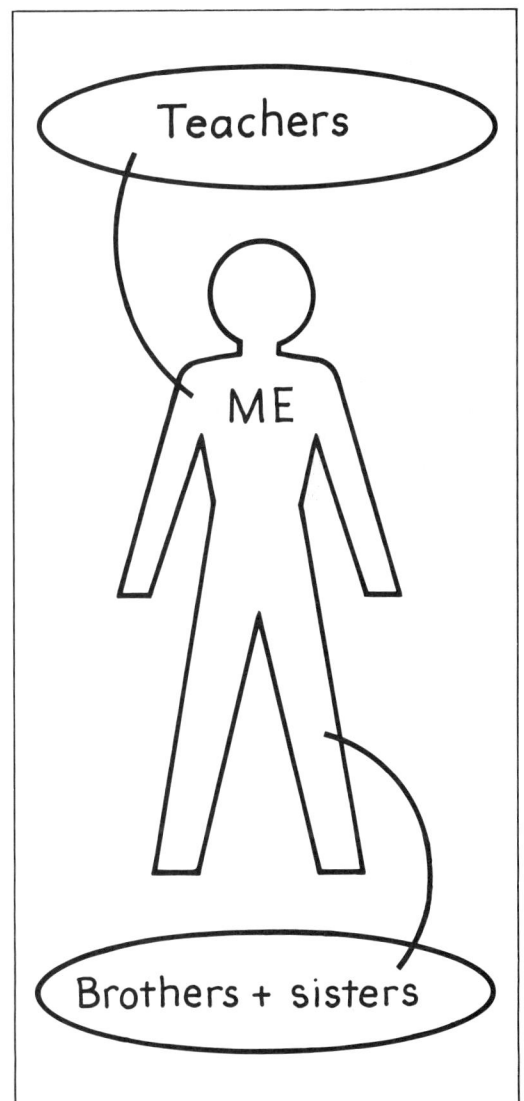

Teachers

ME

Brothers + sisters

DENISE

This passage was written by a 14-year-old girl called Denise, on the subject 'who am I?'

I think I am a very small fish in the middle of a big ocean. There are so many people in the world that you can never say that you are a big fish in a small ocean. You have to think that if you were never born then it would not change anything, and everything would continue as normal. All humans are born to die at some time and that is the only thing which is the same about everyone.

Different people see humans in different ways. Scientists, chemists and politicians all have different ideas as to what humans are. Humans are animals with intelligent brains and a distinct superiority over all other animals. Depending on your ideas, you may think that humans are the ultimate in creation who control their own destiny, or maybe they are just pawns on a chessboard who are just on earth to fulfil certain requirements.

DISCUSSION

1 What do you think Denise means by the following comments?
- 'maybe they are just pawns on a chessboard . . .'
- 'people control their own destiny . . .'
- 'you have to think that if you were never born, then it would not change anything, and everything would continue as normal.'

2 From reading this passage, how do you think Denise feels about the world as she sees it?

3 Do you share any of the thoughts Denise had about the individual and about the world?

4 Are there any ideas in this passage with which you disagree? If so, say which ones, and say why you disagree with them.

HEROINES AND HEROES

Work in pairs.

1 Who is the person (alive or dead) you most admire? What are the things you like and admire about this person? Is there anything about them that you don't like? In what ways would you wish to be like this person?
Tell your partner the answers to these questions.

2 Whether or not you agree with your partner's choice of hero(ine), argue against it, saying why this might not be a good choice of person to imitate. Make your partner justify his/her choice.

DISPLAY WORK

Write a passage about the person you have chosen under the heading 'MY HEROINE' or 'MY HERO'. Include the things you admire about them and the things you do not like. Display your work, and read the work of other members of the class.

GROUP WORK

In your groups, discuss the 'heroes' and 'heroines' displayed. Which ones did people in your group admire the most?

3 AIRPORT !

■ *THINK ABOUT WHY PEOPLE SOMETIMES LIKE TO GO INTO RELIGIOUS BUILDINGS, AND WHAT SORT OF PLACES GIVE PEOPLE A SENSE OF PEACE AND QUIETNESS.*
■ *EXPLORE WAYS OF EXPRESSING IDEAS AND BELIEFS THROUGH ART AND SYMBOL.*
■ *THINK ABOUT THE ROLE OF A RELIGIOUS LEADER, AND ALSO LOOK AT WAYS IN WHICH MEMBERS OF DIFFERENT FAITHS SOMETIMES COME TOGETHER.*

INTERNATIONAL AIRPORT

Chris Bishop is a vicar with a difference, because his parish includes Stansted Airport in Essex, and he works there as Airport Chaplain. The people in Chris's parish include 2000 airport workers and the millions who use the airport every year.

Many new buildings are being constructed at the airport and there are plans to build a chapel which will be open all day and all night. Chris has his own ideas as to what sort of place the chapel should be – he wants it to be a place where people can go to find peace and quiet – a contrast to all the noise and bustle of the airport. He also wants it to be a place where people of any religious faith (or of no faith at all) feel welcome. He has plans for making the focal point of the chapel a large tapestry which will reflect two important themes:

- world air travel;
- the many religions around the world.

This passage from Psalm 139 is one which Chris often uses in services at Stansted Airport.

> Where shall I go from your spirit;
> or where shall I flee from your presence?
> If I climb up to heaven you are there;
> if I make my bed in the grave, you are there also.
> If I fly on the wings of the morning;
> or alight in the uttermost parts of the sea,
> Even there your hand shall lead me;
> and your right hand shall hold me . . .

TASKS

1 Why do you think that some passengers about to make a journey by air might want to spend some time in the chapel?

2 Suppose you were an architect, and Chris Bishop came to you and asked you to design the new chapel for Stansted Airport. Draw your design, taking into account the sort of place Chris wants.

3 Design the tapestry, according to Chris's requirements, which is to be the focal point of the new chapel.

4 Read the passage from Psalm 139 carefully. Why do you think Chris chooses to use this passage so much? Do you think that this passage could have meaning for people of any faith, or of no faith at all?

CHRIS AS AN INDUSTRIAL CHAPLAIN

Stansted
Airport
Chaplain

Here is the emblem of Chris's local group of industrial chaplains.

Chris Bishop belongs to a group of specially trained priests and ministers called *industrial chaplains*.

An important aspect of Chris's job is that he is working with people who may be called upon to deal with any sort of emergency, accident or disaster – this could be anything from a fire to a plane crash, a hijack or a terrorist bomb.

People who work in the emergency services need support. Chris says that part of the job is 'just being there' when he is needed, but sometimes airport chaplains are required to do very difficult and upsetting things, like comforting people who are badly injured, breaking bad news to relatives and being with them as they identify the dead.

Here is the emblem of the Airport Chaplains' association.

TASKS

1 In times of crisis, Chris is expected to be able to give the kind of support which other people could not give. Why do you think this is? Try to find out about ways in which his training might help him to do this.

2 Heathrow and Gatwick airports also have chapels and airport chaplians. Which religious groups use Gatwick Airport Chapel?

GATWICK † ✡ AIRPORT ☪ ☬ CHAPEL 1986

THE CHAPEL is situated in the terminal, on level 3, immediately above the passenger check-in desks.

It is normally open day and night as a place of quiet, mediation and prayer.

CHAPLAINS :

The Reverend P P Bloy   (Anglican; also acting for the Free Churches)

   (Telephone Nos: at Airport, 50-3857
                   at Home, Crawley 28106)

The Reverend M S Hill   (Roman Catholic)

   (Telephone Nos: at Airport, 50-3851
                   at Home, Crawley 22577)

SOME EVENTS

Passengers and staff are welcome at any of these connected with their particular Faith. All the Christian occasions are ecumenical.

January 6 (The Epiphany)	1245 - 1315	Epiphany Service, with carols
March 22 (Saturday)	1015 - 1230	East Grinstead Jewish Community : Worship
March 26 (Wednesday)	1245 - 1315	Service of preparation for Good Friday and Easter Day
March 28 (Good Friday)	1245 - 1315	A meditation within the period of the "Three Hours" on the cross
April 6 (Sunday)	1900	Sikh Community (Crawley): Evening Service
April 25 (Friday)	2030	Jewish Community (Crawley): Sabbath Evening Worship
May 8 (Ascension Day)	1245 - 1315	A Service of Celebration
May 11 (Sunday)	1500 - 1700	Pakistan Muslim Welfare Association (Crawley): Prayers
May 19 (Whit Monday)	1245 - 1315	A service celebrating Pentecost
October 19 - 26 (Daily, exc.Saturday)	1245 - 1315	Silent Prayer. Week of Prayer for World Peace
October 21 - 22 (Tuesday - Wednesday)	2200 - 0730	Vigil : for Racial Peace and Justice
23 December (Tuesday)	1245 - 1315	Service of Preparation for Christmas, with carols

* *

3 People of different religions do not usually share a common building. Why do you think that people seem happy to share a common building at an airport when they would not normally do so? What do you think are the advantages and disadvantages *for religious people* of sharing a building?

4 TIMES OF TROUBLE

■ THINK ABOUT THE PART RELIGION HAS TO PLAY IN TIMES
OF GREAT DISASTER; WHY MANY PEOPLE TURN TO RELIGION
IN TIMES OF TRAGEDY; HOW A WHOLE NATION CAN SUPPORT
A GROUP OF PEOPLE WHO HAVE SUFFERED A DISASTER.
■ CONSIDER HOW PEOPLE FEEL ABOUT TRAGEDIES, HOW
THEY TRY TO MAKE SENSE OF DISASTER, AND HOW
SYMBOLS, SYMBOLIC ACTIONS, SACRED TEXTS AND SONGS
CAN BE USED TO EXPRESS FEELINGS.

DISASTER – CAN THE CHURCH HELP?

On 6 March 1987 the cross-channel ferry *Herald of Free Enterprise* sank just after leaving Zeebrugge in Belgium. Nearly 200 people died, making it Britain's worst maritime disaster since the *Titanic* sank in 1912. The event was one which, apart from bringing tragedy into the lives of many families, stunned the whole of the country.

It is at such times of tragedy that people who may not normally think of themselves as 'religious' turn to religion. The newspaper reports from the time show how deeply involved in the tragedy the Church became, and how the Church tried to offer comfort to those who lost family and friends.

Read carefully the two accounts of services held at Zeebrugge and at Canterbury Cathedral.

Ferry dead mourned at ecumenical service

Relatives of those who died in the *Herald of Free Enterprise* and some of the hundreds involved in the rescue came together in the Roman Catholic Church of St Donas in Zeebrugge yesterday for a short memorial service to honour the dead and comfort the bereaved.

Among the 20 family members brought to the church by coach were some who had only recently identified their relatives among the 53 bodies lying in a makeshift mortuary nearby.

For some, the words of comfort and hope were too much to bear. One collapsed and had to be helped from the church; another was almost too shocked to move. Many were weeping.

The Bishop of Bruges, who led the service with the Bishop of Dover, admitted that it was 'so hard to find the words' to comfort them. 'We don't yet understand what happened or why it happened,' he said. 'We pray for those still missing.'

The Bishop of Dover talked of the 'immense pain which will not quickly be healed. There are no words that can helpfully be used at such a moment as this,' he said. 'There is a natural human tendency always to look for something light and hopeful, but on occasions such as this everything seems dark and there is nothing to sustain our faith and hope. But we do have things for which to be grateful, even in this present darkness.'

He thanked the Belgian people for their love and help. 'In the midst of tragedy our little dreams crumble and seem no longer to be of great importance, and we begin to think of other people,' he said. 'I am told that even in the midst of disaster men and women were holding on to one another. Will we ever get over the shock and pain?'

He addressed the victims' relatives as 'my sisters and brothers who are weeping'.

'I will try to say some words but it is very hard to find them,' he said. 'My voice is silent. My heart is weeping but my eyes remain open. I see the sorrow, the despair, but I also see the cross of Jesus Christ.'

The two bishops, who read the final blessing together, read messages from the Archbishop of Canterbury and the Pope expressing their grief at the tragedy.

The ecumenical service was conducted in Flemish, French and English. The lesson, 'Let not your heart be troubled', was read by Sir Jeffrey Sterling, chairman of P & O, which owns Townsend Thoresen.

The Belgian Coastguard and Navy, which played such a vital part in the rescue, were represented.

There will probably be a larger service in Bruges Cathedral in a few weeks' time. For now, the 30-minute memorial service in a small brownstone church overlooking the busy port of Zeebrugge gave everyone involved a chance to reflect on 60 hours of disaster and despair.

(from *The Guardian*, 10 March 1987)

Runcie leads mourning for ferry victims

By John Ezard

'I hope those of you who have suffered loss may be able to take these words home and keep them close to your troubled hearts,' the Archbishop of Canterbury, Dr Robert Runcie, told next-of-kin of the Zeebrugge disaster yesterday. 'The words are: "Many waters cannot quench love, neither can the depths drown it."'

The service, held as 13 bodies arrived back in Britain and 20 more were identified in Belgium, filled all 1650 seats in Canterbury Cathedral with relatives, survivors and rescue workers. Over 700 bereaved came, including 17 members of one family.

They began to arrive, eyes tired with grief, three hours beforehand. A single muffled bell tolled them into the building, the cradle of English Christianity.

There, at the climax of the sermon meant 'to put into words of a direct and simple character the sympathies of a nation' Dr Runcie said to them: 'Many waters have not quenched your love for those who died. How much less shall the waters quench God's love for them, the God who gave them power to live and be yours – and who gave you the power to love them.

'Those who died at Zeebrugge did not die deserted by God, abandoned by him in an alien element, far away from his care and love.'

Two survivors, Bosun Terence Ayling and Assistant Purser Steve Homewood, slowly walked the length of the nave to lay a memorial

wreath of carnations and freesias at the altar. Four tall Easter candles were placed around it by clergy who, like some of the choir, looked overwhelmed by the emotion of the event. The ferry captain, Mr David Lewry, sat with members of his crew.

The opening hymn, 'For Those in Peril on the Sea', provided the service's hardest moment for next-of-kin and survivors. Next came unusual music for a British service, the piercing Russian Contakion for the Departed, with its refrain, 'weeping over the grave, we make our song'.

With sturdy tenderness the purple-robed Bishop of Bruges, one of 35 Belgian guests, read a lesson from Revelations: 'God shall wipe away all tears from their eyes and there shall be no more deaths.'

Some mourners even managed to sing the next hymn, 'Praise my Soul, the King of Heaven'. Then Dr Runcie rose to open the most obviously meditated sermon he has delivered since his inauguration at Canterbury seven years ago.

Recalling that somebody in the midst of things at Zeebrugge had said, 'Tragedy does not take away love – it increases it,' he went on, 'perhaps we are all more loving people, more sensitive, more concerned for each other, because of that moment of grief which overthrew our ideas of what things matter and opened our eyes again to the importance of our common humanity.'

For some mourners the question was bound to arise, 'Why should a good God let it happen?' But God was not a god who stood outside us and sent disaster, or offered comfort from a distance. 'It is in the selfless heroism of so many at Zeebrugge that we can see God's love at work.'

(from *The Guardian*, 16 April 1987)

DISPLAY WORK

You will need . . .
a traditional hymn book, a bible and a concordance.

1   Make a collage of the hymns and readings used at both services. (Use a concordance to help you find the readings referred to in the articles.) Also write down examples of what the Bishop of Bruges and the Archbishop of Canterbury said on these occasions.

2   The articles refer to a number of rituals, symbols and symbolic actions at the services. Add details of these to your collage, with illustrations where possible.

DISCUSSION/WRITTEN WORK

1   We are told that the purpose of having religious services was:
    – to honour the dead;
    – to comfort the bereaved.
    From what you have learnt about the services, explain how the dead were honoured. What aspects of the services do you think might have offered comfort to the bereaved?

2   The main memorial service in England was held at Canterbury Cathedral, and was led by the Archbishop of Canterbury.
    a) Why did the journalist call Canterbury 'the cradle of English Christianity'?
    b) Find out about and explain the position and function of the Archbishop of Canterbury.
    c) Why do you think the service was held at Canterbury Catherdral? What was this fact trying to *say* to people?
    d) It is perhaps unlikely that all the 1650 people who went to Canterbury attend Church regularly. Why do you think they went to this service? What might they have hoped to get out of it? (There are probably a number of reasons.)
    e) You will have included in your collage a number of things which the Archbishop said. Which of the things he said do you think are central to the Christian message?

TWELVE MONTHS LATER

Arrange your collage of extracts under the following headings:

1 RETURN TO ZEEBRUGGE

Flowers in a bitter wind for victims of Zeebrugge

By John Ezard

Moored over the shallow place where corporate neglect and the sea took their dead a year and a day ago, 270 relatives bereaved in the Zeebrugge disaster said a goodbye of fathomless grief to them yesterday.

In contrast to last April's national memorial service at Canterbury Cathedral, the final commemoration was held outside the harbour's sea wall in a workaday ship, the *Baltic Ferry*, which does the passenger run between Felixstowe and Zeebrugge.

The vessel was a troop ship during the Falklands conflict. And – as the Falklands next-of-kin did in 1983 – yesterday's mourners of the worst British civilian maritime catastrophe since the *Titanic* gathered at their own request to cast flowers on the 30-foot waters where it happened.

They were flown to Ostend by P & O, went by coach to Zeebrugge, and made the 23-minute journey from the town on a ferry's upper car deck, converted into a makeshift chapel, in the middle of a mile-wide exclusion zone patrolled by a Belgian frigate to give them privacy.

There they joined in a gesture of solace which, though they had to drop their wreaths through the modern ventilation ports of the ferry deck, was as old as antiquity. Two children threw flowers with a card inscribed 'Daddy, Miss You' as a thin skirl of voices sang the hymn 'Praise my Soul, the King of Heaven' in a biting wind.

A family of six put their arms round each other as they cast their flowers. An old lady leaned on a relative and a walking stick, hobbling in procession towards the window. Two children threw single red roses. A woman lifted a toddler to do the same. It took 20 minutes to bestrew all the flowers.

(from *The Guardian*, 7 March 1988)

2 A HERO REMEMBERS

The most solitary tribute was by Mr Andrew Parker, who was awarded the George Medal for acting as a human bridge. A Belgian tug took him and his daughter Janice, 13, alone to the waters of Zeebrugge, where they cast 193 single flowers into the sea – one for each of the dead.

Afterwards Mr Parker said: 'I could see it all happening again before my eyes, the screams of terror and the ice-cold water. Coming back has been very painful. But something made me return. I had to thank the people of Belgium. I still feel guilty about being alive.'

(from *The Guardian*)

Earlier brave Andrew Parker, the 'human bridge' who saved two lives, paid his own private tribute.

Andrew, a 34-year-old London bank executive, sailed out of the harbour on the tug which was the first rescue vessel at the disaster scene. He and his 13-year-old daughter Janice tossed 193 blooms into the sea . . . one for each victim.

Later he joined the memorial service at Dover where he lit 193 candles.

'The memories still haunt me,' he said. 'But after this I feel more at peace.'

(from the *Daily Mirror*)

Mr Andrew Parker, who received the George Medal for his heroic efforts in the Zeebrugge disaster, lighting candles with his family at St Mary's parish church, Dover, during yesterday's memorial service.

3 REMEBRANCE SERVICES

A TOWN OF TEARS REMEMBERS

By Barry Wigmore and Graham Barnes

They arrived in ones and twos for the service and stood quietly looking up at the new stained glass window commemorating that terrible day a year ago.

Some blinked away tears, some wept openly. Then they took their places in St Mary's, the flint and limestone Norman church close to the sea at Dover.

Captain David Lewry, skipper of the doomed crew, was there with his wife Patricia. He controlled his emotions until the Bishop of Dover, the Right Rev Richard Third, started his sermon.

The Bishop told the congregation: 'You cannot go on living in grief . . . there must come a time when you stop crying.'

Captain Lewry sobbed. But his tears went almost unnoticed by the others. Their sorrow was spilling over, too.

Four-year-old Timmy Perkins, orphaned by the disaster, was a forlorn little figure, but he did not cry. His grandmother Sheila Payne, who now looks after him, said proudly: 'He is the bravest boy in the world.'

Above the congregation, the memorial window shone out peace. Designed and crafted by artist Frederick Cole, it depicts Christ stilling the waters and includes those who helped during the disaster.

Nearly 200 seamen – many still on strike – marched in silence to Dover town centre to pay tribute to the victims.

(from the *Daily Mirror*)

A commemorative roll of honour, listing the names of the disaster's victims, was unveiled in front of the memorial window, which cost more than £10,000.

The Bishop of Dover said in his address, which was relayed to crowds outside the church and reverberated across Dover: 'Who needs this window? I believe it is most needed by those who most deeply sorrow, for you cannot go on in an agony of grief.'

Many of those who could not bear to go were among 700 who attended a service yesterday at St Mary's Church, where a stained glass window to the dead was unveiled. The artist, Mr Frederick Cole, said: 'I lived for a moment in the minds of those people who drowned.'

(from *The Guardian*, 7 March 1988)

Survivors and grieving families were warned at a memorial service yesterday that unresolved feelings about the sinking of the *Herald of Free Enterprise* a year ago could poison their lives.

In an emotional service on board a ferry moored at the exact spot where the *Herald* capsized just outside the Belgian port of Zeebrugge, over 250 mourners were urged to make the anniversary a new beginning.

The Rev Peter Bowers, of St Peter's and St Paul's Church, Dover, said: 'You may feel anger, bitterness, resentment and even, perhaps, guilt. If it is not possible now, I urge you in the months and years to come to forgive, otherwise these feelings will poison your lives.'

(from *The Times*, March 1988)

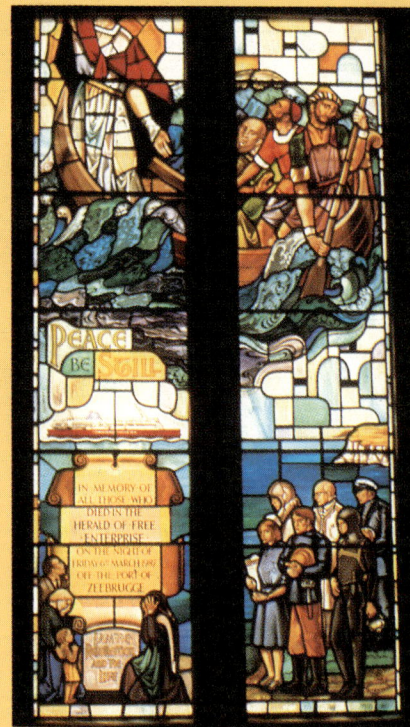

In memoriam . . . part of the stained glass window dedicated in St Mary's Church, Dover, to the Zeebrugge dead

WHY RETURN?

Why do you think so many people wanted or even needed to go back to the scene of the disaster? In what ways might it have been helpful to them?

REMEMBRANCE

1 Andrew Parker said that after returning to Zeebrugge and attending the service at Dover, he felt 'more at peace'. What do you think he meant?

2 One of the hymns sung at the remembrance service was also sung at the service a year previously at Canterbury. Which hymn was it, and why do you think it was chosen?

3 The Rev Peter Bowers said that people may feel anger and resentment. Against who might they have such feelings? He went on to say that these feelings could poison people's lives. What do you think he meant?

THE WINDOW

1 A 'roll of honour' listing the victims' names was unveiled under the stained glass window. The word 'honour' appears a number of times in the articles on Zeebrugge. What does it mean? Why might it be important to the bereaved that the dead were 'honoured' in this way?

2 The designer of the window said: 'I lived for a moment in the minds of the people who drowned.' How do you think this might have helped him design the window?

3 In what ways might this window help the bereaved?

4 Draw your own design for a window in memory of the dead at Zeebrugge.

SYMBOLIC ACTIONS

Look for examples of symbolic actions performed during the two remembrance services. Write about these actions, with illustrations. Add them to your collage. Explain what these actions and symbols may have meant to different people.

DISCUSSION

1 'It's at times like this it's good to know that the Church is there.' Give your reasons for agreeing or disagreeing with this statement.

2 Considering the Church's participations in the events surrounding the disaster, can you think of any non-religious group or individual who could have done as much for the survivors, rescuers and bereaved?

3 The articles you have read illustrate many of the feelings experienced by people who survive this sort of disaster and by those who are bereaved. Make a list of these feelings. Do you think these feelings are common aspects of bereavement?

4 Some people do not like the idea of the Church being presented as 'coming to the rescue' in times of crisis. They say it makes the Church look like 'the elastoplast of society'.
   - What do you think the person meant by 'the elastoplast of society'?
   - Do you think that part of the Church's task IS to be 'the elastoplast of society'?

5 WHAT'S THE POINT ?

*YOU WILL BE LOOKING AT HOW ONE PERSON TRIED TO FIND
A CAUSE THAT WOULD MAKE LIFE WORTH LIVING.
YOU WILL BE THINKING ABOUT WHAT IT MEANT TO LIVE A
LIFE FULL OF MEANING, AND THE IDEA THAT EVERY LIFE
HAS A PURPOSE.*

THE SEARCH FOR MEANING

People often talk about looking for the MEANING or PURPOSE in life. They may be looking for the things which make life worthwhile – those things that make life worth living.

In the extract (right) from *The Chosen* by Chaim Potok, the Jewish community in America are just hearing the first broadcasts on the radio telling them the full extent of the sufferings of Jews in Europe under Hitler.

RESEARCH

Find out (if you do not know already) what happened to the Jewish people under Hitler.

QUESTIONS TO THINK ABOUT

1 From the passage you have read, how do you think Reb Saunders' view of the 'purpose of life' was different from that held by Reuven's father?

2 From what Reuven's father says, what do you think he might do with his own life to give it meaning and purpose?

DISCUSSIONS

1 Discuss within your group things which you might do which would give meaning and purpose to your lives.

I sat in a chair and listened, and when the news programme was over my father turned off the radio and looked at me.

'How is Reb Saunders?' he asked quietly.

I told him what Reb Saunders talked about that afternoon.

My father nodded slowly. He was pale and gaunt, and his skin had a yellowish tint to it and was parchmentlike on his face and hands.

'Reb Saunders wanted to know how God could let something like this happen,' I told him quietly.

My father looked at me, his eyes somber.

'And did God answer him?' he asked. His voice had a strange quality of bitterness to it.

I didn't say anything.

'Did God answer him, Reuven?' my father asked again, that same bitterness in his voice.

'Reb Saunders said it was God's will. We have to accept God's will, he said.'

My father blinked his eyes. 'Reb Saunders said it was God's will,' he echoed softly.

I nodded.

'You are satisfied with that answer, Reuven?'

'No.'

He blinked his eyes again, and when he spoke his voice was soft, the bitterness gone. 'I am not satisfied with it, either, Reuven. We cannot wait for God. If there is an answer, we must make it ourselves.'

I was quiet.

'Six million of our people have been slaughtered,' he went on quietly. 'It is inconceivable. It will have meaning only if we give it meaning. We cannot wait for God.' He lay back on the pillows. 'There is only one Jewry left now in the world,' he said softly, staring up at the ceiling. 'It is here, in America. We have a terrible responsibility. We must replace the treasures we have lost.' His voice was hoarse, and he coughed. Then he was quiet for a long time. I saw him close his eyes, and I heard him say, 'Now we will need teachers and rabbis to lead our people.' He opened his eyes and looked at me. 'The Jewish world is changed,' he said, almost in a whisper. 'A madman has destroyed our treasures. If we do not rebuild Jewry in America, we will die as a people.' Then he closed his eyes again and was silent.

2 Imagine that you were an American Jew living at that time, and that you had just heard for the first time the full extent of the horrors of the concentration camps in Europe. How do you think you would have felt? What questions about God and about the human race would you have had to ask?

6 BECAUSE IT'S THERE

YOU WILL BE THINKING ABOUT THOSE THINGS WHICH GIVE PEOPLE A SENSE OF SATISFACTION AND ACHIEVEMENT – THOSE THINGS WHICH OFFER A CHALLENGE – AND YOU WILL BE CONSIDERING WHY PEOPLE FEEL A NEED TO ACHIEVE AND BE CREATIVE.

The cheetah is running after its prey because it needs to eat. For the cat, running to catch its food is like going out to work for a human being.

Steve Cram does not *have* to run for a living. So why do he, and hundreds of other people, spend their time trying to run faster, jump higher, or throw further than anyone else? Some people do make their living these days from sport, but this does not on its own account for their desire to break records and win races.

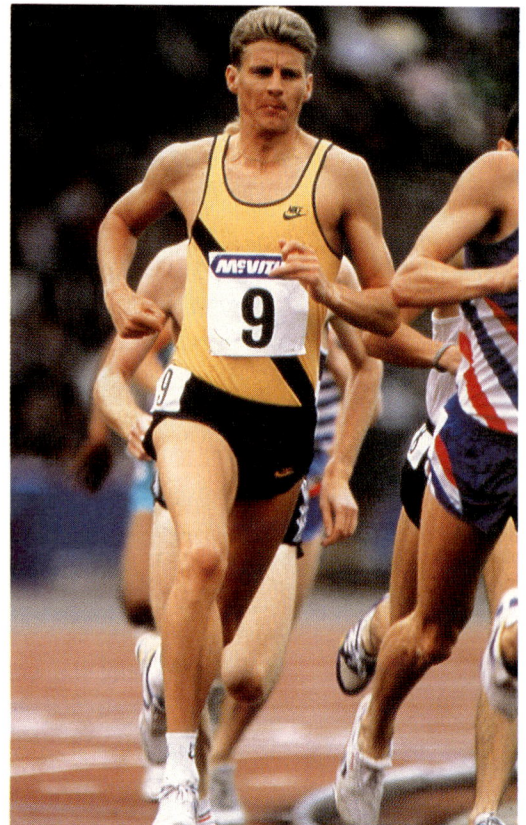

ACTIVITY

Make a list of all the things you can think of that people do for their own satisfaction, or as a challenge. It may be something to do with sport (such as running a marathon in your personal best time), or it may be to do with collecting, or reaching a high standard on a musical instrument, or making something beautiful – or many other things besides. If you have time, you could make a collage of the ideas you have collected. What title might you give your collage to show other people what it is about?

Look at your list or collage. Taking each activity in turn, ask yourselves the following:
- Why do I think people get pleasure out of doing this? (There may be a number of reasons in each case.)
- Do I think it is a worthwhile way of spending time?
- Do other people enjoy watching this activity? If so, for what reasons?

THE MEN, THE WOMEN AND THE MOUNTAIN

Often a mountaineer can't explain any more clearly the reason for what she or he does. Doug Scott, co-leader of the team who attempted to climb the North-East Ridge of Everest in 1988, talks (below right) about the task ahead of them.

Dougal Haston on the summit of Everest in 1975; photograph taken by Doug Scott.

WHY DO YOU WANT TO CLIMB EVEREST?

BECAUSE IT'S THERE.

WORD SEARCH

Scott uses a number of words and phrases in the article extract which may help explain why he and his team are climbing the mountain.

1 Find any words or phrases which suggest that what they are doing involves difficulty and hardship.

2 Find words and phrases which suggest that the task needed considerable preparation.

3 Find a word which suggests that in spite of all the preparation, there was still an element of surprise in the task.

4 Find words which suggest that the team had a strong sense of excitement and expectation before they set out.

Suffering breathlessness and headaches on the last stage of the journey up to 21,000 feet, we were revived on having our first post-monsoon view of our ridge. After following a moraine highway through ice pinnacles, we turned a corner and the whole of the North-East Ridge and face was there in its entirety, so unexpected after months of planning and years of dreaming. Having seen the ridge from the other side of such peaks in Nepal as Makalu and Baruntse it was so good to see our objective right in front of us.

Crazy, isn't it, that a four-mile, snowed-up, rocky, pinnacled ridge could hold that kind of fascination for us. We looked up though binoculars and telephoto lenses, working our way up the heavily corniced ridge, wondering how we would negotiate the rock steps and how we would turn the pinnacles that had defeated three previous expeditions and where our friends Peter Boardman and Joe Tasker disappeared on Chris Bonington's expedition of 1982. And beyond the pinnacles at least a mile of ridge to go to the summit, all of it above 8000 metres, and then how would we get down?

. . . So here we are, a comparatively modest team all fit and well, looking forward to some climbing after months of planning, travelling and acclimatising. With our ages ranging from 24 to 46, and a team originating from Austria, the USA, India, England and Scotland, there are guaranteed interesting times ahead in terms of our feelings for each other as much as for the intrinsic interest of finding a way to conquer this, the last major unclimbed feature of Mount Everest.

(from *The Guardian*, 1988)

MY GREATEST ACHIEVEMENT

'What has given you the most satisfaction in life?'

A group of teachers was asked this question. They all had at least one university degree, and all held senior posts in their schools. Look at some of the answers they gave:

What do you notice about their answers? Are they the answers you would expect from this sort of group?

Learning to ride a bike when I was 40.

Giving birth to my children.

Passing grade 8 on the oboe when I was 32. I had always wanted to play the instrument but when I was at school my parents couldn't afford to buy me one.

Watching the seeds I sow come up.

The day I was confirmed.

SURVEY

- Now ask the following question to three people – an adult, someone your own age and YOURSELF.

  'What has given you the greatest satisfaction in life?'

- Display the answers you get in two lists headed ADULTS and TEENAGERS. Leave space beside each answer.
- Are there any differences between the two lists?
- Now look at the list of words in the shaded box.

DREAMING	FASCINATING	SURPRISE
CRAZY	PREPARATION	COMRADESHIP
DIFFICULTY	INTERESTING	EXCITING

- Beside each of the answers on your lists, write down any of the words from the box which you think might apply to that particular achievement. (For instance, was the achievement something that might have involved a lot of difficulty, or preparation etc?) Think about your own greatest achievement so far. Which of the words in the box apply to it?

RECORD BREAKERS

In your groups, look through the *Guinness Book of Records*. If you were to spend a lot of time in your life working towards breaking just one of these records, which would it be, and why? Make a display showing what records the members of your group would most like to break, and say why.

What do you think the chances are of any of your group members breaking these records?

7 ACHIEVEMENT

YOU WILL BE ASKING WHAT QUALITIES AND ACHIEVEMENTS PEOPLE SHOULD BE AIMING FOR IN LIFE, AND THINKING ABOUT HOW YOU COULD DESCRIBE DIFFERENT STAGES IN THE ACHIEVEMENT OF THESE QUALITIES.

How do you know how you are getting on at school? Who describes how much progress you are making – you? – your friends? – your teachers?

It may be that you still have the old-fashioned type of school report which has a list of subjects down the left-hand side, and against each subject an exam mark and a grade for effort. However, it is very likely that you take home from time to time some sort of PROFILE or RECORD OF ACHIEVEMENT. This will probably be a document in which comments are made about your achievements under a number of headings.

The headings show what sort of things are valued by the school and regarded as important. BUT . . . just suppose that someone – somewhere – was keeping a record of our achievements in the 'School of Life'. After all, many religions do teach that at the end of our lives we will be judged according to our deeds in this world.

If our achievements in this life were recorded in this way, what headings might be used? Would they be the same as your school record? Maybe it would be more important to be assessed on your wealth, or beauty, or kindness to hedgehogs!

RECORD OF ACHIEVEMENT IN THE SCHOOL OF LIFE

1 Make a list of six areas in which you think people should be assessed, looking at their life as a whole.

2 Now the difficult bit; many profiles describe a number of levels at which you can achieve in one area. For example, if you said that 'kindness to hedgehogs' was one important area in which people should be judged, your three levels might be:

level 1 . . . runs over hedgehogs on sight;

level 2 . . . screeches to a halt when hedgehog is sighted;

level 3 . . . goes round putting up notices saying 'HEDGEHOG CROSSING POINT'.

Taking your six areas of achievement, work out three levels for each of them.

3 Let every group *research* ONE religion. If a person of that faith believed that they would be judged on their achievements in six areas of life, what might those six areas be?

8 POTENTIAL

YOU WILL BE CONSIDERING THE IDEA OF POTENTIAL, AND THE POSSIBILITIES THAT LIFE OFFERS – OF HOW IT IS POSSIBLE TO ACHIEVE UNEXPECTED GOALS EVEN OUT OF DISASTER – OF HOW, IF WE ARE TO MAKE THE BEST USE OF THE POSSIBILITIES OFFERED BY LIFE, DIFFICULTIES USUALLY HAVE TO BE OVERCOME.

POTENTIAL – SCHOOL REPORT

Alice has worked very hard this term. Her work shows considerable sensitivity towards the feelings of others and I feel that she has the potential to follow a career which involves working with people. However, if Alice is to fulfil this potential she will need to organise her work better, remembering that exam qualifications are necessary for the course she wants to take at College . . .

- If you were Alice, would you take these references to your POTENTIAL as a compliment?
- What does 'potential' mean?
- What does it mean when someone says that you have 'fulfilled your potential'?
- What does Alice have the potential to do, and what does she need to do to fulfil that potential?

COLLECT . . . if you can

. . . quotations from reports people in your tutor group have received which use the word 'potential'. Look at them carefully. If you do not have any examples, ask some of your teachers what potential they think you have.

1 What is each report saying about the pupil?

2 In each case, what will the pupil have to do to fulfil their potential?

3 In each case, is it just up to the person concerned to fulfil their potential, or will they need help from others if they are to do so?

POTENTIAL – THE CHILD

Adults talk a lot about children and young people having potential. We all have skills, knowledge and powers which we can use in ways which will benefit others, or in ways which will be harmful to others. It is widely agreed that how we 'turn out' as adults depends very much on how we are brought up as children. Look at the cartoon and read the caption.

DISCUSSION

- What is the boy doing, and what feelings do you think he is expressing
- What is the meaning of the shadow behind him?
- Talk about what the cartoon and caption mean.
- Do you think that the message of the cartoon is always correct?
- What could be done to prevent it happening?

GROUP STORY WRITING

In groups of four or five, write a story about the boy in the cartoon. The first person in the group starts by writing (or speaking into a tape recorder) about how the boy's day began. Then the second person takes over and builds up the story to include an account of what happened before the boy picked up the stone. The third person takes up the story from the time when the boy picked up the stone, and tells about how the boy felt and what he wanted to do. The fourth person then tells how the incident ended. There are two possibilities:

a) the boy could throw the stone – what happens next?

OR

b) the boy changes his mind, puts the stone down and finds another way of coping with his feelings.

If there are five people in your group, the last two people should produce the different endings, (**a**) and (**b**).

'The child is the father to the man.'

· POTENTIAL ·

CARTOON TIME

Draw your own cartoon to illustrate the idea of potential. Make your subject a child who develops his/her potential for better or worse.

POET'S CORNER

Write a poem to illustrate your cartoon or the one on page 32. You could begin with the birth of the boy and write a passage showing him after every five years, illustrating how he develops if no one checks his behaviour. How might he turn out? How might his story end?

POTENTIAL DENIED

You may have read *The Diary of Anne Frank,* whose Jewish family hid in an attic (the Annex) in Amsterdam during World War II in an attempt to escape Nazi persecution.

Read the following passages. One is an extract from the book, the other an article about the Anne Frank House Museum.

During that night I really felt that I had to die, I waited for the police, I was prepared, as the soldier is on the battlefield. I was eager to lay down my life for the country, but now, now I've been saved again, now my first wish after the war is that I may become Dutch! I love the Dutch, I love this country. I love the language and will not give up until I have reached my goal.

I am becoming still more independent of my parents, young as I am, I face life with more courage than Mummy; my feeling for justice is immovable, and truer than hers. I know what I want, I have a goal, an opinion. I have a religion and love. Let me be myself and then I am satisfied. I know that I'm a woman with inward strength and plenty of courage.

If God lets me live, I shall attain more than Mummy ever has done, I shall not remain insignificant. I shall work in the world and for mankind!

And now I know that first and foremost I shall require courage and cheerfulness!

Yours,
Anne

The Frank family were betrayed. Anne, her sister and her mother all died in concentration camps shortly before the end of the war. It would be helpful for you and your group to find out more about Anne Frank and to read other parts of her diary.

The Anne Frank House

The place where Anne wrote her diary is now a museum, called the Anne Frank House.

After the war the canal house in which Anne and her family had hidden for so many months fell into disrepair. In 1957 the Anne Frank Centre was set up. One of its primary objectives was to restore the house to its former state. From that time on, people have been able to visit the Annex and to see for themselves the place where the family hid out.

There are exhibitions too. These are put on to show things Hitler wanted. Even in today's world, there are still people who are persecuted. There are still people whose lives are being made unbearable, just as Anne's was. It seems as if everyone has already forgotten all that happened during World War II.

The Anne Frank Centre preserves the Annex, but it does not only want to look to the past. By means of educational projects, seminars, press releases and the like it tries to stimulate the fight against anti-semitism, racism and all the current forms of fascism.

DISCUSSION

1 From what you have read, what would you say were Anne's main goals in life?

2 What things about herself does Anne most value?

3 Had she not died, what sort of person do you think Anne would have been when she grew up? What do you think she might have been able to do with her life?

4 Anne wanted to work for the world and for mankind. Did she achieve her goal? If so, say in what ways?

- Have you ever wished that you could start your life all over again, but that this time round you could take back with you all that you have learnt about the world so far?
- If you could start life again, what are the dangers you would know to look out for? What problems will you have to face? What could help you face these things?

Read this poem by Louis MacNeice. It is not an easy poem, and you may not understand every word, but try to understand what the poem as a whole is about.

Here are a few of the more difficult words and phrases with their meanings.

DRAGOON – force   LETHAL AUTOMATON – deadly robot
DISSIPATE – waste   ENTIRETY – wholeness

PRAYER BEFORE BIRTH

I am not yet born; O hear me.
Let not the bloodsucking bat or the rat or the stoat or the
    club-footed ghoul come near me.

I am not yet born; console me.
I fear that the human race may with tall walls wall me,
    with strong drugs dope me, with wise lies lure me,
        on black racks rack me, in blood-baths roll me.

I am not yet born; provide me
With water to dandle me, grass to grow for me, trees to talk
    to me, sky to sing to me, birds and a white light
        in the back of my mind to guide me.

I am not yet born; forgive me
For the sins that in me the world shall commit, my words
    when they speak me, my thoughts when they think me,
        my treason engendered by traitors beyond me,
            my life when they murder by means of my
                hands, my death when they live me.

I am not yet born; rehearse me
In the parts I must play and the cues I must take when
    old men lecture me, bureaucrats hector me, mountains
        frown at me, lovers laugh at me, the white
            waves call me to folly and the desert calls
                me to doom and the beggar refuses
                    my gift and my children curse me.

I am not yet born; O hear me,
Let not the man who is beast or who thinks he is God
        come near me.

I am not yet born; O fill me
With strength against those who would freeze my
        humanity, would dragoon me into a lethal automaton,
            would make me a cog in a machine, a thing with
                one face, a thing, and against all those
                    who would dissipate my entirety, would
                        blow me like thistledown hither and
                            like water held in the
                                hands would spill me.

Let them not make me a stone and let them not spill me.
Otherwise kill me.

DISCUSSION/WRITING

When you have read the poem, discuss the following:

1   The poem is called a prayer. Make a list of the words in the poem which tell you that it is a prayer.

2   Who is saying the prayer, and to whom might they be praying?

3   The writer expresses many fears about what is ahead of him/her. Make a list of these fears, but leave space beside each one. *(verse 2)* Then write an explanation of what you think each of these fears is about.

4   List the things which the writer thinks will help him/her to cope with the difficulties ahead. *(verse 3)* How could these things be of help?

5   In verse 4, the writer suggests that during our lives we often become involved in activities which we would rather not do.
   a)   How can 'they' murder by means of *your* hands? Who might 'they' be? Can you resist 'them'?
   b)   What other sins can 'the world' commit through you, or any of us?

6   Imagine that you could go back and start life again, taking with you all of your present knowledge and understanding. Write your own 'Prayer Before Birth'. Include the fears which YOU would want to be guarded against, and those things which you feel will help you cope with the world. You could also include 'prayer' for the things in life which give happiness.

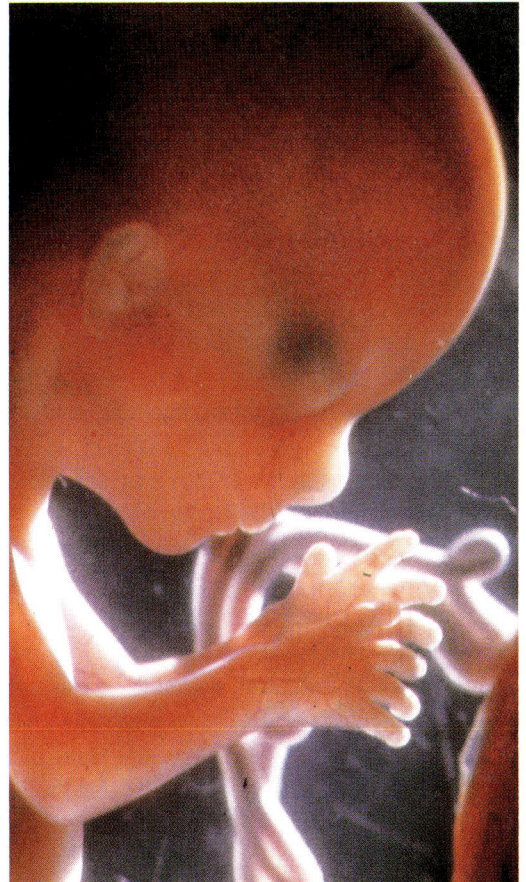

9 | WHAT'S THE ANSWER ?

YOU WILL BE LOOKING AT HOW RELIGIOUS BELIEFS GIVE LIFE MEANING AND OFFER ANSWERS TO LIFE'S QUESTIONS FOR SOME PEOPLE – AND AT HOW OTHER PEOPLE EQUALLY FIND MEANING IN NON-RELIGIOUS BELIEFS AND PHILOSOPHIES.

FINDING MEANING IN BELIEF

We interviewed five people and asked them if their beliefs, religious or otherwise, helped make sense of life for them, or gave meaning to life. They may not have answered in the same way that someone else holding similar beliefs would have done, but they do say what their beliefs mean to them.

MIRIAM (Orthodox Jew)

'My religion is very important to me. For a start, it gives me a great sense of belonging to a people who can trace their history back to the beginning of the world.

'My religion teaches that we, the Jewish people, have a special purpose. The Almighty's purpose has been revealed through our law. We may not understand it all, or understand what the Almighty's purpose is, but we know that part of His purpose is that we obey His commands. This idea – that everything has a purpose – does help make sense of life for me. I suppose it seems that accepting the Almighty's purpose even though I don't know what it is doesn't seem to answer anything. But if you think about it, which of us can say why evil things happen, like the terrible things that have happened to the Jews? Other people may just shrug their shoulders and say, "It's terrible, I don't know why it happened," but I at least can find some comfort in believing that there IS a purpose and so everything that happens must have meaning that is known to Him and is part of His divine plan.

'I feel that I have a place in the world and I know what that place is. I see other teenagers standing at street corners, kicking cans in the gutter, looking thoroughly bored. I can't help thinking that they'd be happier if they had some sense of identity – not just with the gangs who ride their bikes around the North Circular, but with a great tradition that has stood the test of time, that will stay with you all your life, and pass on to your children and grandchildren.'

ASHOK (Hindu)

'How does my religion give meaning to life? I suppose I would say that my religion *is* the meaning in my life and of my life. I get my values and priorities from the teachings of my religion. These teachings have been handed down by wiser men than I, and I see no reason to question them. I only wish to carry them out as well as I can.

'I see my religion as a very personal thing. Yes, coming together at the Temple with others is important, we are a very spread out community and there are many people who I only see once a week. But for me, worship at the Temple on Sundays does more to remind me that I am Indian than strengthening my spiritual life. That comes through my own private meditation when I learn to be one with, and at peace with, myself and the world.

'I do believe that if I do well in this life then I will benefit at my rebirth. But I don't try to live a good life just to be rewarded – I believe that it is important to treat all people in the world – and indeed the world itself – with respect.'

Jo (Christian)

'I became a Christian at the age of 16, after what I can only call an inner feeling that Jesus was calling me to follow him. I think there are two ways in which my faith helps me to make sense of life.

'Firstly, I belong to a church – Roman Catholic, as it happens. I love to go to Church on Sundays. After the week at school with all the arguments, homework, rushing around – to have a chance to spend two hours devoting myself to God, and strengthening my relationship with Him is pure luxury. I do pray at home, or out on the street, or anywhere, but with people banging on the bathroom door or the noise of the traffic, it's not the same.

'I regard my life in this world as a preparation for the next. I think that one of the most important things about being a Christian is that it makes you realise that however clever you think you are, you can never know even a fraction of all there is to know – and you can't even secure your own salvation. Not one of us can ever be perfect enough to be regarded as "good" in God's eyes, for His standards are so much higher than ours. We can't do it alone, and this is why God sent Jesus into the world, to set an example of how God wants us to be and to prepare the way for us to heaven by dying to make up for our sins.

'Religion is a way of life, so it has to give meaning and purpose to everything you do. I live my Christian life every day, aware that Jesus set certain standards for me to follow in my dealings with other people. It's not easy – but making the effort is a lot more satisfying than just living for yourself, or wandering through life aimlessly with no purpose.'

LIZ (feminist)

'I've been a feminist for as long as I can remember, and part of the women's movement since my late teens. I believe that society needs changing. At the moment it's run *by* men, *for* men, with *men's* interests at heart. This affects *all* women, whether they realise it or not – at home, at school, in religion and in the job market. Black women are particularly badly off.

'I'm not religious. In fact, I don't believe in God. But if I did, I'd say that I found it in the midst of my women friends. It's all about support and understanding and having someone to turn to when it all gets too much. When I get really depressed I read Mary Daly or Susan Griffin. Then I feel strengthened and ready to continue fighting for those issues that affect me.

'People often ask me "why do you bother?". I usually reply that I don't have a choice.'

SIMON (scientist)

'I was brought up a christian, and although I have gone through the times of doubt that everyone has, I've remained in the Church for the 25 years of my life. I studied engineering at university, and now I work for a big computer company. People are often surprised at how many scientists are "religious". I don't find it odd at all! Scientists tend to like order and design. There is no one I can admire more than the architect of the wonderful universe we live in. People sometimes call engineers and scientists "inventors". That is not strictly true. We actually *discover* things. We didn't invent electricity – we simply discovered that it existed and found out how it could be used. Everything we do depends on powers and substances which are already there – and we certainly didn't put those things there!

'I believe that God is the creator of all things. I don't mean He went "ZAP!" and made the world in seven days, but that He (or She) set the whole thing in motion for some reason which we do not yet understand. I am very aware of my place – a very SMALL place – in the wider universe. I am also only too aware of how limited we people are in what we can do, however great seem to be our achievements.

'Of course, I can't PROVE that God is there in the way that I can prove certain scientific facts. That is what people find difficult to understand – and I can't blame them – that people who have experienced God in their lives can never PROVE it to others, they can only say that the presence of God is something that they feel within them.

'The Holy spirit is my guide – always there to give me strength. I may not be able to see, touch or smell Him, but I have other senses which detect His presence.'

STATEMENTS ABOUT HOLDING A BELIEF

- **My beliefs give me a strong foundation on which to build my life.**
- **My beliefs help me get myself in proportion compared to the rest of the universe.**
- **My beliefs help me to learn the will of God.**
- **My beliefs give me something to live for.**
- **What I believe, and how I act now, has an effect on my next life.**
- **My beliefs have stood the test of time.**
- **I get my values in life from my belief.**
- **I get a sense of peace from my beliefs.**
- **My beliefs tell me that there is meaning in life.**
- **My beliefs give me a strong sense of belonging to a culture.**
- **My beliefs bring me close together with others and strengthen my sense of belonging.**

ACTIVITIES

1 Above is a list of statements about holding a belief. Make a grid with the statements down one side and the names of the five characters in this unit alone the top. Discuss in your groups which of the statements might have been made by any of the five characters. Put a tick against a statement under the name of anyone who you think could have said it. Which statements about holding a belief did you think were the most commonly held among our six characters?

2 Discuss in your groups if there are any statements about holding a belief which one or some of the five characters might have made. If so, add it to the grid.

3 Carry out your own survey among people you know who hold strong beliefs. Show them the list of statements and ask them to choose the five which they agree with most. Ask them if they would like to make one new statement themselves about the importance in life of holding a belief.

As a result of your inquiries, what would you say were the most important aspects of holding a belief or belonging to a religion?

4 **'SEEING WITH MY EYES' game**

This game is to be played in groups of up to six people.

You will need . . .

some card in two different colours. Each set of cards is for one group.

Using colour A, make up six cards – all the same size. Write one of the following names on each card:

MIRIAM ASHOK JO LIZ SIMON

Using colour B, make at least six 'statement' cards. (After you have tried the game out, you can make more cards with other statements on.) Print one of the following statements on each card:

'Belonging to a religion and holding beliefs is for really stupid people.'

'Holding a set of beliefs is just an excuse for belonging to a large group. It's okay if you are insecure, but it's much better to break free from groups and find out what you believe for yourself, rather than follow someone else's teaching.'

'The only reason why religious people try to live a good life is so that they "go to heaven" or get a good reincarnation or whatever their religion teaches. If there's no life after death, then trying to live a good life will have been a waste of time, won't it?'

'What I say is – live for yourself – put number one first. If you don't, no one else will.'

'There is only one all-powerful supreme being in the Universe that we know of, and that is MAN!'

'There is no purpose in life. Things happen because we make them happen. There is no *reason* for it all. We are born, we live, we die. That's it.'

How to play

Game 1: each player takes two cards – one of each colour – without letting other players see what they have. You have to work out how the person on your name card would respond to the statement you have drawn. You should take 5-10 minutes to work this out properly.

Each person reads out their situation and then says what they think their 'person' would say about it. The others in the group have to try and guess which character is speaking.

Game 2: play in pairs. Each pair takes ONE statement card and TWO character cards. Again you will need time to work out how your character would respond. Discuss the statement you have drawn with your partner, each of you taking the part of one character on your selected cards.

QUESTIONS TO DISCUSS

1 Those people interviewed were asked to talk about what gave life MEANING. What does this actually mean? What would a life that had no 'meaning' be like?

2 Most of those interviewed suggested that it is important to have a set of principles by which to live your life.
   a) Do you agree?
   b) Are there any sets of beliefs which you consider would be very unsuitable as the basis of living one's life?

3 Ashok said that worshipping at the Temple did more to remind him that he was Indian than strengthen his spiritual life.

a) What do you think he meant?

b) Taking other examples known to members of your group, in what ways do you think religion can strengthen a person's sense of cultural identity?

4 Liz lives by a firmly held set of beliefs which are not religious.

a) What other set of beliefs by which people live their lives are not religious? Think of as many as you can.

b) Think of as many similarities and differences between Liz's beliefs and those of the 'religious' people interviewed as you can.

5 Simon says that many scientists are religious, and explains why he thinks this is the case.

a) How might you find out if there is any tendency for scientists to be religious?

b) Discuss the reasons Simon gives as to why scientists might be expected to be religious.

6 Here are some ideas which come out of the interviews. Discuss whether you agree or disagree with them, and give your reasons.

- A religion which has lasted for hundreds or thousands of years has to be taken seriously.
- Everything that happens in life has a reason or purpose.
- Life in this world is a preparation for the next.

SUMMARY

Of all the points made by the people interviewed in this unit, which single point interested you, or made you think the most? Compare your answer with those of the rest of your group, making sure that you all explain carefully the reasons for your choice. Display your responses and look at those of other groups.

WHY?

A good way to vary your discussion is to write the statements for discussion on separate cards. Everyone in the group takes a card and has to give their opinion on what it says. Everyone else in the group listens very carefully, and whenever one of them thinks that the person speaking has not given a good reason for what they are saying, asks 'WHY?' The speaker should then try to give a reason for what he or she has just said.

SEVEN AND A HALF MILLION YEARS LATER

'Alright,' said Deep Thought. 'The Answer to the Great Question . . .'
   'Yes . . . !'
   'Of Life, the Universe and Everything . . .' said Deep Thought.
   'Yes . . . !'
   'Is . . .' said Deep Thought, and paused.
   'Yes . . . !'
   'Is . . .'
   'Yes . . . !!! . . . ?'
   'Forty-two,' said Deep Thought, with infinite majesty and calm.

(from *Hitch-hiker's Guide to the Galaxy* by Douglas Adams)

This answer (not surprisingly) did not satisfy anybody! But as the computer explained, they hadn't asked the right question, and therefore couldn't expect a satisfactory answer!

In the first unit in this book, you were asked to write down what you thought were the most important questions about 'Life, the Universe and You'. Here are some of the questions asked by someone else. Read them carefully. Are any of them the same as yours? What answers would you give to them?

Who am I?   Where do I belong?   What am I really like?
What is the most important thing I believe?   What do I believe in?
To what do I feel most committed?

Why am I like I am?   Why do I act towards others like this?
Why do I regard this as being important?   Why do I value this experience?
How do I make decisions?

What/who shall I be?   What is my purpose?   What is my value?
What seems to be worth dying for?   Can I change?
Should I change?   How do I feel about myself?

GCSE NOTES FOR THE TEACHER

The three books in this series have been written specifically for use in Religious Education, but they will also be an invaluable resource for teachers of Integrated Humanities, PSE and sixth form general studies. The books are marked by **three fundamental characteristics:**

OPEN-ENDED AND FLEXIBLE

You will find that they can cover each unit in brief in as little time as two weeks, or in depth and by adding ideas of your own in as much as half a term. There is no assumption made that all pupils will engage in all activities, and in fact the books were not designed to be 'text books' to be followed through from beginning to end. Rather, these materials might become 'dippers' to which pupils can turn in the course of their studies to extend their skills and abilities. Most pupils can attempt most of the work in the books. The assignments and activities have been compiled especially to enable pupils of different ages and abilities to respond at their own level.

LEARNING BY THINKING

These books have not been written to convey knowledge of facts. The books are ACTIVITY books, for those lessons where teacher input will be at a minimum with pupil involvement taking a high profile – the teacher acting in an advisory capacity. It is hoped that teachers will use this material in conjunction with a unit of work on a related topic, and that pupils will work at the activities with a certain amount of knowledge gleaned from elsewhere.

The advent of GCSE has placed greater demand on UNDERSTANDING and EVALUATIVE skills. Many teachers are looking for material which will develop these abilities in years 2–5, and this series will meet this need. A number of activities in these books may prove useful as the basis of coursework assignments and have been labelled with this symbol: ▶K▶U▶E▶ – knowledge, understanding and evaluation.

GCSE ASSESSMENT OBJECTIVES

The National Criteria for Religious Studies do not at present answer the question 'What must candidates be able to DO in order to demonstrate ability in the areas of understanding and evaluation?' Teachers who have puzzled over this in the setting of appropriate coursework may have reached some of the following conclusions:

- Abilities demonstrative of **understanding** involve offering explanations as a result of following through certain processes:
  a) ANALYSIS – this involves breaking down an overall mass of evidence into its constituent elements and where necessary re-constituting elements by means of classification.
  b) INTERPRETATION – ascribing meaning and significance. This skill is particularly appropriate to Religious Education.
  c) APPLICATION – being able to apply what is known to particular circumstances.
  d) EMPATHY – the ability to differentiate one's own response from that of others, and to appreciate the differences between one's own values, beliefs etc. and those of others.

- EVALUATION is largely a matter of *making a personal judgement/response.* Pupils are expected to weigh up arguments using the appropriate evidence.

GCSE — THE FIELD OF STUDY

These books concentrate on the area of study common to all syllabuses and currently prescribed by the National Criteria under the heading of **UNDERSTANDING** (see Assessment Objectives 3.2.1–3.2.5). These areas of study may be summarised as follows:

Candidates should demonstrate knowledge and understanding of:

a) the language, terms and concepts of religion;
b) the concept of AUTHORITY enshrined in sacred texts, special people, and the tradition of religions;
c) the principal BELIEFS of the religion(s) studied;
d) MORALITY – religious and non-religious responses to contemporary moral issues, both personal and social;
e) ULTIMATE QUESTIONS – identification of those questions beyond which no further questions are possible. A consideration of selected responses to those questions.

Underlying these categories is a sixth – that of EXPRESSION – the means by which belief is expressed through language, story, symbol, art, music, literature, ritual etc.

HOW DO THESE BOOKS FIT IN WITH GCSE?

Book 1: What Do You Think?

. . . is mainly concerned with looking at moral issues and how they are resolved, and especially with the question of the relationship between belief and behaviour.

Book 2: Life, the Universe, and You

. . . explores some of the key questions encountered in life, and in particular looks at the ways in which different people find meaning and purpose in life.

Book 3: Ways of Saying

. . . explores:

- some of the ways in which people experience the presence of what they may (or may not) call God;
- some of the ways in which people, and particularly certain religious faiths, have expressed their beliefs and experiences through art, music, architecture, poetry etc.

RESOURCE LISTS

As units will be used within the context of work on a given theme, a list of recommended resources for each unit is given on the next page. Teachers and pupils should also be looking for other stimulus materials in newspapers, magazines etc.

RESOURCES

You will find the books listed here will give you more information on the themes explored in the book. There are also organisations who will send you information if you write to them. Remember you should always enclose a stamped addressed envelope.

1 That's life

Hitch-hiker's Guide to the Galaxy by Douglas Adams, Pan
Gospel According to Peanuts, Coronet Books/Hodder & Stoughton
Charlie Brown, Coronet Books/Hodder & Stoughton
pictures, magazines, postcards

2 Who am I?

Religious Education and Human Development by Michael Grimmitt, McKrimmon

3 Airport!

Some research material in World Religions, e.g. *Shap Handbook on World Religion*
World Religion in Education, Commission for Racial Equality

4 Times of trouble

hymn book, bible, concordance

5 What's the point?

The Chosen by Chaim Potok, Penguin
Churban by Tony Bayfield, published by Michael Goulston Education Foundation

6 Because it's there

REACH (your own school record of achievement)
Guinness Book of Records

7 Potential

The Diary of Anne Frank, Pan Books
Anne Frank in the World – Uitgeverji Bert Bakker, Amsterdam 1985
Louise MacNeice Collected Poems, Faber

8 What's the answer?

Christian World; Jewish World; New Religious World etc; published by MacDonald

Gingerbread, 35 Wellington Street, London WC2E 7BN
Samaritans
Unemployed group
(see your British Telecom telephone directory for local groups of the above)

Community Service Volunteers, 237 Pentonville Road, London N1 9NJ
National Council for Voluntary Organisations, 26 Bedford Square, London WC1B 3HU
Greenpeace, 30-31 Islington Green, London N1 8BR
Intermediate Technology, 9 King Street, London WC2E 8HW
World Wide Fund for Nature, Panda House, Godalming, Surrey GU7 1QU